Get
Acquainted
With
Your

Bible

Gary L. Ball-Kilbourne

INTRODUCTION

In this introduction you will get a taste of

- what the Bible is
- why the Bible is important
- how the Bible came to be
- what is in the Bible
- how the Bible tells about God
- how to use your Bible

Does the Following Describe You?

Many adults know less about the Bible than they wish. Some reasons they give include

— I never took Sunday school seriously;

— I thought the Bible was boring, irrelevant, and/or too difficult to understand;

— I left the organized church for years and have just now come back.

Spurred by a desire to know more about God and to belong to the people of God—the church— many of these same adults want to discover what the Bible offers.

If you are one of these adults, think of this book as a sampler. Read the chapters. Take a quick taste of morsels from the Bible. And come away, perhaps not completely satisfied, but knowing you want to taste more.

Quick Facts

 17% of all American adults report they read the Bible daily.

 23% report they read the Bible weekly, at least during congregational worship.

20% say they have never read the Bible.

 27% of American Protestants report they belong to a Bible study group.

61% of American Protestants are able to name at least one of the four Gospels.

The Bible Is . . .

Did you know that the modern English word *Bible* comes from an old Greek word literally meaning "books"? That fact gives us a clue to discovering what the Bible is. Books make up the Bible—more than one book. As you browse through your Bible, you will find sixty-six quite diverse books.

What other names do you or others call the Bible? These names can help you uncover facts and beliefs about what the Bible is. For example, many Bibles have the title "Holy Bible" printed on the cover. The word *holy* says that something is set apart from the ordinary and associated with the divine. Or, some persons call the Bible "the book of the people of God" or "the church's book." These names imply that through the Bible, God makes God's self known to the people of God in a special way.

The Bible...

tells us who God is and how God relates to God's people.

In the Bible, God's people tell the stories about how they have encountered God. They tell how they have met God in creation, in liberation, in judgment, in the coming of the Christ into the world. Their stories reveal for us who God is and how God relates to God's people.

Why Some Books Made It into the Bible . . . And Some Did Not

Did you ever hear of The Gospel According to Thomas? the Letters of Clement? the Shepherd of Hermas? the Didache? These Christian books were written about the same time as the books that make up the New Testament, but they did not make it into the Bible. What happened to them?

While some writings, such as a third letter of Paul to the Corinthians, have apparently been lost, the writings named above are still around. You can find copies translated into English in religious research libraries. However, decisions were made around the fourth century to consider some writings in addition to the Old Testament sacred but to exclude others. Why were some kept and others not?

Fourth-century church leaders decided which writings would be standard Christian Scriptures based on

—the soundness of their teaching;
—their association with one of the first apostles;
—their general usage throughout the church of that time.

Some decisions were controversial. The Shepherd of Hermas almost made it into the Bible because of its sound doctrine and widespread usage. However, it was not associated with an apostle. The Revelation, which was associated with the apostle John, almost was not included in the Bible because of its strange, difficult imagery.

The "canon"—the official list of books considered authoritative as Scripture—was finally closed around the end of the fourth century. However, some Christians even today wonder if that was a wise decision. The Holy Spirit, they say, might speak clear, fresh words of significance to Christians through other, perhaps new, writings.

How the Gospel of Luke Came Into the Bible

1. The disciples observe Jesus teaching.

2. A disciple tells the story of Jesus orally to others.

3. As the first generation of disciples dies off, persons begin writing down the story of Jesus.

4. Luke, using at least two written sources as well as things he had heard, writes his Gospel in Greek, probably to share with the Roman official Theophilus [thih-AHF-ih-luhs].

5. Luke, or Theophilus, shares Luke's Gospel with other Christians.

6. Over the next three centuries, Luke's Gospel is copied, passed around, and collected with other writings.

7. In the fourth century, Christian bishops and councils decree that the thirty-nine books of the Old Testament plus twenty-seven Christian books—including Luke's Gospel—are "canonical" or standard writings for official, authoritative Christian use.

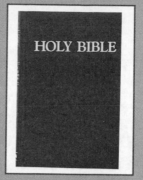

Cover

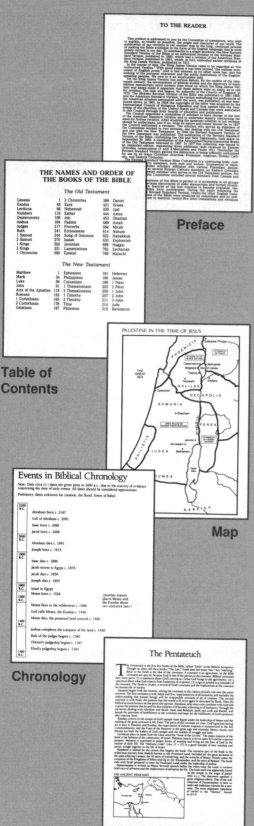

Preface

Table of Contents

Map

Chronology

Introduction to Major Section

Meet Your Bible

Take your Bible in hand. Look on its **front cover** or **spine**. Somewhere it will say what version— what translation or paraphrase—it is. This book uses the New Revised Standard Version, first published in 1989, for its Bible references. You might be looking at a *Good News Bible*, a New International Version, or a King James Version.

Many Bibles begin with a **preface** or **introduction** telling how the version came to be. Read the preface if you are curious about how the Bible moved from manuscripts written in ancient Hebrew and Greek to the English language of your Bible.

Inside your Bible, after the title page, you should find a **table of contents**. This table lists the books within the Bible in their order, divided into two major groups—the Old Testament and the New Testament.

Some people like to memorize the books of the Bible in order, so they will always have an idea where to look in their Bible for a certain book. If you dislike memorizing, you can always check the table of contents to find out on which page Ruth, Isaiah, Romans, or some other book begins.

Some Bibles have **maps**. When you come to a place name in a Bible story, you can locate it on a map. A map can show you that it is about seventeen miles from Jericho to Jerusalem.

Some Bibles have **chronologies** or **time lines**. These tools can help you discover that Moses lived roughly 250 years before King David and that David ruled Israel for about 45 years some 10 centuries before Jesus was born.

Some Bibles offer brief **introductions to books** or **major sections**. These introductions share important background information about when and why books were written and what major themes they contain.

Other helps might be found in your Bible, depending on its edition.

Thumb through your Bible. What helps does it offer you?

WARNING: Not an Easy Read

Some persons become quickly discouraged when they attempt to read the Bible. They find many portions of the Bible difficult to understand. In fact, many sections of the Bible are almost incomprehensible to today's American Christians. Not all these sections are vitally important for the modern reader to grasp. For example, much of the legal code contained in Leviticus is irrelevant to today's situations. However, other passages urgently need to be read and yet are difficult to understand.

Some bits of advice when reading the Bible becomes difficult:

▶ Don't give up.
▶ Try to gain a sense of the major themes of the Bible before attempting to work through the Bible verse by verse. This book will point out some of those themes.
▶ Work with a group or class on problem sections.
▶ Try using Bible study tools, such as
Bible dictionaries—to look up names, words, customs, and concepts
Concordances—to find what verses contain a particular word
Bible atlases—to look up places on maps
Commentaries—to read what scholars think about certain Bible passages.
▶ Use your imagination to envision yourself among the participants in the Bible story or among the first readers of the Bible passage.
▶ Ask your pastor for help.

As you read the New Testament, for example, remember that the world was different for a first-century Palestinian Jewish Christian than it is for you. Do you talk and think in Aramaic? Do you believe that the world is flat and that spiritual beings called demons cause illness? Do you sell wares in a dusty marketplace? herd sheep on foot? cast a net for fish by hand from a sail-driven boat?

Reading the Bible is always a cross-cultural experience. But by learning about another time and place and by using your imagination, Bible study can become alive and fascinating.

Old Testament

God's Covenant of Law With the People of Israel

Major Section	Books	Major Contents
Pentateuch ("five scrolls") TORAH "THE LAW"	Genesis, Exodus, Leviticus, Numbers, Deuteronomy	Creation; early Hebrew heroes; exodus from slavery in Egypt; covenant and law at Mount Sinai; wandering in the wilderness; laws and ordinances
History "FORMER PROPHETS"	Joshua, Judges, Ruth, First and Second Samuel, First and Second Kings, First and Second Chronicles, Ezra, Nehemiah, Esther	Conquest of Canaan; rise and fall of the kingdoms of Israel and Judah; exile in Babylonia and return
Poetry and Philosophy "THE WRITINGS"	Job, Psalms, Proverbs, Ecclesiastes, Song of Solomon (Song of Songs)	Wise writings about faith and life; hymns of praise, prayers; love songs
Major Prophets (longer prophetic writings)	Isaiah, Jeremiah, Lamentations, Ezekiel, Daniel	God's words of judgment and hope
Minor Prophets (shorter prophetic writings)	Hosea, Joel, Amos, Obadiah, Jonah, Micah, Nahum, Habakkuk, Zephaniah, Haggai, Zechariah, Malachi	God's words of judgment and hope

New Testament

God's Covenant in Jesus Christ With All People

Major Section	Books	Major Contents
Gospels	Matthew, Mark, Luke, John SYNOPTIC similar in writings	The life and teachings of Jesus Christ written differently
History	Acts of the Apostles	The church is born and spreads
Letters Primarily written by Paul Some by Peter	Romans; First and Second Corinthians; Galatians; Ephesians; Philippians; Colossians; First and Second Thessalonians; First and Second Timothy; Titus; Philemon; Hebrews; James; First and Second Peter; First, Second, and Third John; Jude	Teaching, advice, and encouragement to churches established
Apocalypse (revealing "that which is hidden")	Revelation	God's final victory

Read It for Yourself

Several passages in the Bible speak about the purposes and uses of the Bible.

① Read John 20:30-31. What purpose for the writing of John's Gospel does this brief passage indicate?

② Given that John's Gospel was probably written for Christians in the city of Ephesus around the year 100, after most of the first generation of Christians had died, why did the author seek to accomplish his purpose by writing about the "signs" that Jesus did?

③ Read John 20:24-29. What advantages did Thomas have over later generations of Christians, including yourself?

④ Read 2 Timothy 3:14-17. Keeping in mind that there was no New Testament when Second Timothy was written, what were the "sacred writings" and "scripture" to which Paul referred?

⑤ What types of usefulness did Paul claim for Scripture?

Let the Bible Form You

Most modern Christians start to read a Bible passage with the assumption that they will "get something out of it." Often, this means they attack the text in their Bible study, bringing to bear every tool at hand, seeking to mine from it nuggets of information and wisdom. While studying the Bible in this way offers rewards, alone it does not satisfy the deeper spiritual yearnings of the human being.

For example, in studying Psalm 119:105-112, you might find the information interesting that this passage is from the Bible's longest psalm (176 verses!), that Psalm 119 forms an acrostic with each stanza beginning with a different letter of the Hebrew alphabet, and that this poem is a prayer in praise of God's law. However, unless reading Scripture somehow serves to form a person's inner self, bare information becomes mere trivia.

Each chapter in this book will include an opportunity for you to permit Scripture to form you within, instead of merely informing you. For example, take a few minutes each day for a week to

▶ Pause and ask God to allow the words of Scripture to work within you.

▶ Read Psalm 119:105-112 aloud or silently.

▶ Pause to reflect on one small portion of the passage, whatever part attracts you, allowing God's Spirit to lead your thoughts.

▶ Ask God to use those words and thoughts to mold you more closely to God's will.

▶ In the spirit of Psalm 119, give thanks to God for revealing God's self to you through the Bible.

▶ Sing or hum the psalm response printed below.

Thy word is a lamp un-to my feet____
and a light un-to my path.

CHAPTER 1
GOD
YEARNS
FOR A
PEOPLE

In this chapter you will

👉 look at the biblical accounts of how God created human beings in God's image

👉 consider the story of the first sin and what sin has meant for relationships between humanity and God

👉 contemplate the depth of God's yearning for a people

God Creates Human Beings

Genesis gives two accounts of God creating human beings. The two accounts offer different specifics.

Genesis 1:26-31	Genesis 2:4b-10
On the sixth day of creation (when God made land animals)	On the day when God made the earth and the heavens
—humans were made in God's image;	—the first man was brought to life by God's breath;
—male and female were created by God at the same time (no details on how);	—the first man was formed from the dust of the ground with life breathed into him by God; the first woman was made from one of the first man's ribs;
—humans were given dominion over the earth, to fill it and subdue it;	—humans were placed in the garden of Eden to till it and keep it;
—humans were given every plant and tree for food.	—humans were given every tree for food except the tree of the knowledge of good and evil.

What Is the Image of God?

Genesis 1:26-27 says that God created human beings in God's image. What might the "image of God" mean? Here are some theories:

—personhood and personality
  —self-consciousness
    —the ability to reason
      —physical appearance
        —freedom of the will
          —the capacity to create
            —the ability to choose good
              —status as God's agent on earth

Which of these theories appeal to you? Are they equally valid? Why, or why not?

What about yourself is in the image of God?

The Book of Genesis mentions the image of God twice more. Following the story of Cain's murder of Abel, Genesis 5:1-3 repeats Genesis 1:27 and speaks of Adam passing his image on to his son Seth. Following the story of the destruction of the world by a great flood, Genesis 9:6-7 recalls the creation of humanity in God's image as the reason why humans ought not to murder other humans.

Christians believe that sin distorted or even destroyed the image of God that had been created within humanity. At the least, this distortion or destruction means that human beings, left to themselves, cannot avoid sinning. Renewal of God's image became possible, though, through Jesus Christ. New Testament writings such as Colossians 3:10 speak of "the new self, which is being renewed in knowledge according to the image of its creator."

God's Commission to Humanity (Genesis 1:28)

What does God's commission to humanity say about God's yearning for a people?

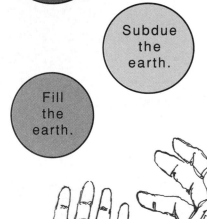

How are you living out God's commission?

What's in a Name?

Adam: from the Hebrew word *adam*, literally meaning humankind; formed from the dust of the ground, which in Hebrew is *adamah*; in Genesis 2–3, *adam* appears to mean the "first man"; *Adam* is not used as a proper name until Genesis 5:1.

all living"; perhaps Eve's name also celebrates the deferral of the death promised to the first humans if they ate of the tree of the knowledge of good and evil.

Eve: from a Hebrew word meaning "to live"; in Genesis 3:20, the first man names the first woman Eve, "because she was the mother of

Eden: from a Hebrew word probably meaning "to delight"; Eden can thus be thought of as "the garden of delight" or "the delightful garden."

Humanity's Sin and God's Judgment, Mercy, and Grace

Immediately after the story of the Creation, the writer of Genesis 2:4b–3:24 turns to the story of the first sin. Here is an outline of the story:

Genesis 2:17 God warns the man that eating of the tree of the knowledge of good and evil will bring immediate death.

Genesis 2:25 The first humans are naked and not ashamed.

Genesis 3:6-7 The first humans eat of the forbidden fruit, have their eyes opened, know they are naked, and sew fig leaf loincloths to cover themselves.

Genesis 3:10 The first humans fear God and hide from God because they are naked.

"Expulsion From Paradise"

Genesis 3:21 God, as a gift of grace and out of God's deep yearning for a people, makes garments of skin to clothe the first humans.

Genesis 3:16-19, 22-24 God, out of mercy and a deep yearning for a people, drives the first humans out of Eden, still alive, though facing lives of hardship before death finally comes.

Make a list...

Read It for Yourself

Read Genesis 2:15-17 and Genesis 3. As you read, make a list of questions you would like to ask.

As a guide to your reflection, consider these questions:

—Why do you think God allowed the first humans to eat of every tree of the garden except the tree of the knowledge of good and evil?

—What means did the serpent use to tempt the woman?

—What do you think the fruit of the tree of the knowledge of good and evil tasted like?

—How did God punish the human beings?

—How did God show God still loved the human beings?

—What was the sin of the first human beings?

(Where might you look for help with your questions? A concordance? A Bible dictionary? A commentary? Your pastor? Or are your questions unanswerable?)

—Who was responsible for that sin?

Choices

Reading from Genesis 2–3, fill in the chart to indicate the choices faced by the first humans and by God.

	First Humans	God
Choices faced in Genesis 2–3	_____ _____	_____ _____
How free to choose?	_____ _____	_____ _____
Connection between choices and consequences	_____ _____	_____ _____
Basic choice underlying all other choices	_____ _____	_____ _____

For Your Eyes Only

These questions are asked to guide your private reflections. You need never share your answers with anyone. However, you might choose to talk about these questions with your pastor or with a trusted Christian friend.

What one choice made by you in the past do you wish you had to make over again?

What were the consequences?

What were your feelings about the choice you made?

How have you made related choices since then?

How have you faced the consequences and feelings arising from your choice?

How did you talk with God before and after the choice?

What choices are you facing now that involve your relationship with God?

How are you dealing with those choices?

Close your time of reflection with the prayer in the margin.

O God,
maker of every thing and
    judge of all that you
    have made,
from the dust of the earth
    you have formed us
and from the dust of
    death you would raise
    us up.
By the redemptive power
    of the cross,
    create in us clean
        hearts
    and put within us a new
        spirit,
that we may repent of our
    sins
    and lead lives worthy of
        your calling;
through Jesus Christ our
    Lord.
                    Amen.

"Ash Wednesday," by Laurence Hull Stookey. Words © 1989 The United Methodist Publishing House. Reprinted from *The United Methodist Hymnal* by permission.

Adam's and Eve's Response to Sin

1 They tried to hide their guilt. (They covered their nakedness.)

2 They tried to run away . (They hid from God.)

3 They blamed someone else. (The man blamed the woman.)

4 They blamed God. (The man complained that it was God who made the woman in the first place.)

5 They blamed nature. (The woman blamed the serpent.)

6 They blamed it on a misunderstanding. (The woman claimed she was tricked.)

The Great Cover Up

"Sin traditionally implied guilt, answerability, and, by derivation, responsibility" (from *Whatever Became of Sin?* by Karl Menninger; Hawthorn Books, 1974; page 20).

Responsibility for our actions does not sit well with most of us. We do not like to admit to ourselves that we have done wrong. Even less do we enjoy opening up our guilt for all the world to see.

We resemble our first ancestors. The first humans tried six strategies to avoid accepting responsibility for the sin of eating from the tree of the knowledge of good and evil.

How have you seen these strategies tried recently in attempts to evade responsibility?

What difference might it make to claim responsibility for our sin?

Let the Bible Form You

Psalm 8 is a hymn of praise commenting on the status given to human beings in Genesis 1:26. The focus is on glorifying God for the glory and power God has given humanity. The lordship God has granted over all other living things places human beings just slightly lower than God. Humanity stands at the pinnacle of God's creating. The creation of humanity is the result of God's deep yearning for a people.

As information, you might be interested to learn that the words translated as "mortals" in Psalm 8:4 are in Hebrew *ben adam*: son of *adam* or child of humankind.

In verse 2, "the enemy and the avenger" do not refer to specific individuals but form a parallel to "your foes" a line earlier. In Hebrew poetry verse is formed, not by rhyming words as in English, but by constructing phrases expressing parallel thoughts or images. The "enemies" of God in this instance appear to be those either who do not believe in God or who follow after other gods. The psalmist says that even the babbling of babies discredits those enemies.

Verses 5-8 marvel that the Creator should desire to share the dignity of authority over creation with created human beings.

Move now to experience how Psalm 8 may form you within. Take a few minutes to do the following:

▶ Pause and ask God to allow the words of Scripture to work within you.
▶ Read Psalm 8 aloud or silently.
▶ Permit the words of Psalm 8 to form images in your mind. Let those words and images take you where they will. Don't be afraid to play with them.
▶ Ask God to use those words and images to mold you more closely to God's will.
▶ In the spirit of Psalm 8, marvel at God's great love for you in sharing lordship over creation with you.
▶ Sing or hum the psalm response printed below.

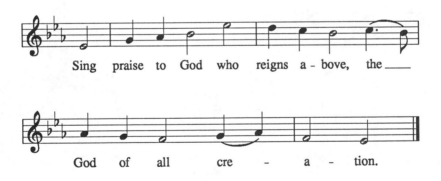

Words by Johann J. Schutz; trans. by Frances E. Cox.
Tune: Bohemian Brethren's *Kirchengesänge*.

CHAPTER 2

GOD
CHOOSES
A
PEOPLE

In this chapter you will

- ☞ meet Abraham and Sarah

- ☞ **learn how God chose Abraham and Sarah to be the first of a chosen people**

- ☞ explore the meaning of covenant

- ☞ consider what faith is

Humanity's Predicament

At the end of the Bible stories covered in Chapter 1, God had evicted the first human beings from the garden of Eden because of their sin. That experience was only the beginning of their troubles.

Murder appeared with the second generation of humans. One son of the first man and first woman, Cain, killed another son, Abel, because of envy. Cain was then exiled by God to wander in another land (Genesis 4:1-16).

Time passed, and things went from bad to worse. Finally, "the LORD saw that the wickedness of humankind was great in the earth, and that every inclination of the thoughts of their hearts was only evil continually. And the LORD was sorry that he had made humankind on the earth, and it grieved him to his heart" (Genesis 6:5-6). God then destroyed the world with a great flood but saved a remnant of humanity and animal life in an ark built by Noah, "a righteous man" (Genesis 6:7–9:17).

Later, humans attempted to build a great city and tower stretching to the heavens in order to glorify themselves. God confused them, however, by scattering them across the earth and by causing them to speak with different languages (Genesis 11:1-9).

Yet God did not give up on humanity. God still yearned for a people.

Biblical history next focuses on the lives of a man and a woman, named Abram and Sarai (later renamed Abraham and Sarah). Tragedy was present in their story due to the fact that Sarai was barren. She had not borne and, at her advanced age, surely would not bear children. Literally, Abram and Sarai faced no future. As far as they were concerned, existence would end when they died. There was nothing toward which to look ahead or for which to work.

Yet God chose to come to this childless, futureless, hopeless couple and to present them with a series of promises. One of those promises was that they would have many descendants. They would become the parents of a chosen people. The stories of Abram and Sarai tell of their responses to God's promises (Genesis 12–25).

This drawing from an Egyptian tomb painting shows a Semitic chieftain, like Abraham, taking his tribe to Egypt around 1900 B.C.

Section of the Royal Standard of Ur, a mosaic showing the Sumerian army about 2500 B.C.

The Days of Abraham and Sarah

Abraham and Sarah lived around the year 2100 B.C. (Before Christ). Keep in mind that the years "Before Christ" are numbered backward, so that the year 2098 B.C. comes forty-seven years before the year 2051 B.C.

To help put the days of Abraham and Sarah into perspective, the time between Abraham's and Sarah's journey to Canaan [KAY-nuhn] and the birth of Jesus is a slight bit longer than the time between Jesus' birth and today.

By the time of Abraham and Sarah
—writing had been used by the Sumerian people in the Mesopotamian region between the Tigris and the Euphrates rivers (modern Iraq) for at least 1,400 years;
—Egypt had been ruled by pharaohs for 1,000 years;
—the first Egyptian pyramids had been built six centuries earlier, and the Great Sphinx had already been constructed;
—a bronze age civilization had emerged on the island of Crete in the Mediterranean Sea;
—ceremonial centers were being built along the sea coast of Peru;
—an urban civilization had existed for 1,000 years in what is now Pakistan and western India;
—astronomy was a fully developed science in Egypt, Mesopotamia, India, and China.

The Travels of Abraham and Sarah

Many of the Bible's stories about Abraham and Sarah tell of their journey from Ur of the Chaldeans [kal-DEE-uhns] to the land of Canaan and of their stops at locations in between. Locate on the map on page 23 some of the places where Abraham and Sarah lived.

Ur [oor]—Ur was located on the Euphrates River in the region known as Lower Mesopotamia, west of the modern city of Basra, Iraq. In the time of Abraham and Sarah, Ur was a major city where a king dwelled and ruled.

Haran [HAIR-uhn]—Haran was a major commercial city in the time of Abraham and Sarah, located north of modern Turkey's border with Syria. Abraham's father, Terah, died there (Genesis 11:32). Abraham's and Sarah's grandson, Jacob, fled to safety in Haran after tricking his brother Esau out of his inheritance (Genesis 27:41–28:5).

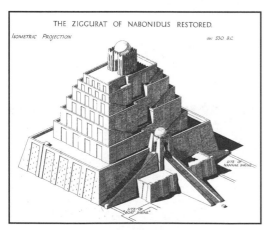

An artist's rendition of the Ziggurat at Ur with the temple of Nannar, the moon god, at the top

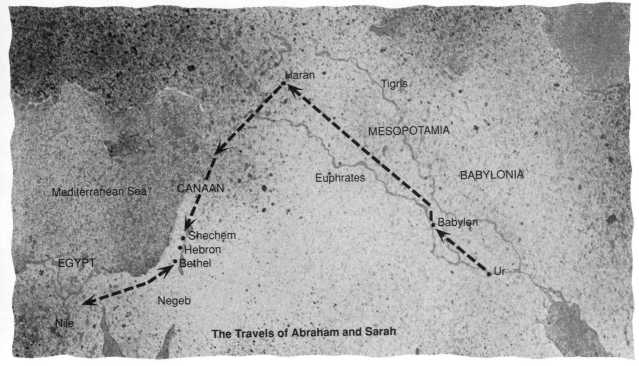

The Travels of Abraham and Sarah

Shechem [SHEK-uhm]—In Abraham's and Sarah's time, Shechem was already an important Canaanite city. It was located in the hill country near Mount Gerizim, about forty miles north of the future site of Jerusalem. Shechem was situated on a major crossroads, lying across the only east-west road through the mountains of northern Canaan. Although Canaanites already lived in this area, Abraham likely first came to understand while living in or near Shechem that here was the land God was promising to him and his descendants.

Bethel [BETH-uhl]—Bethel is mentioned in the Old Testament more than any other city except Jerusalem. It was founded about a century before the time of Abraham as a Canaanite sanctuary city dedicated to the god El. Located about ten miles directly north of the future site of Jerusalem, Bethel was also the site of Jacob's ladder dream (Genesis 28:10-22).

Negeb [NEG-eb]—Negeb literally means "the dry land." Later it came to be understood simply to mean "south." The Negeb is the region of modern Israel situated between Gaza and the Gulf of Aqaba and bordering on the Sinai Peninsula. Although it is a desert region now, in Abraham's and Sarah's time the Negeb held plenty of grass on which animals could graze while traveling between Canaan and Egypt.

Modern city of Shechem

Young camel in the Negeb

What's in a Name?

Throughout the Bible, names carry important meanings. In Chapter 1, you saw the meanings of the names *Adam, Eve,* and *Eden.* In the Bible passages studied in this chapter, you will find that Abraham's name starts out as Abram and Sarah's as Sarai. God changes their names in Genesis 17:1-22. Why?

We do not know one absolutely final reason behind these name changes, except that God decided the changes should be made. However, it might be significant that while Abram means "exalted ancestor," Abraham means "ancestor of a multitude of nations." Abraham's name change seems to emphasize God's covenant promise to make Abraham "the ancestor of a multitude of nations" (Genesis 17:4).

Both Sarai and Sarah seem to mean the same thing: "princess." But an old Jewish tradition holds that this slight shift in name meant that Sarah moved from being a princess only to her own people to become a princess to all people.

Make a list...

Covenant: A Thread Woven Throughout the Bible

"And I will make my covenant between me and you, and will make you exceedingly numerous" (Genesis 17:2).

These words spoken by God to Abraham contain one of the 382 times that the word *covenant* appears in the New Revised Standard Version of the Bible. Besides being one of the most frequently used words in the Bible, *covenant* is also one of the most important.

In fact, the word *testament* that appears in the titles of the two sections of the Bible we call the "Old Testament" and the "New Testament" means a covenant between God and humanity. If we were not already so used to saying "Old Testament" and "New Testament," we could just as accurately call the two major sections of the Bible the "Old Covenant" and the "New Covenant."

Read through Genesis 17, and make a list of verse numbers where the word *covenant* appears.

What can you tell about the meaning of the word *covenant* from its usage in this chapter of Genesis?

We do not often use the word *covenant* in everyday modern English. The closest words in meaning are *contract* and *agreement*, but they do not mean precisely the same thing as covenant means. A contract or an agreement is a deal negotiated by two persons of more or less equal standing with each other. A covenant, as it appears in the Bible, is an arrangement between one who has greater power and one who has lesser power. Moreover, the more powerful party offers the covenant, which the less powerful party evidently has the freedom to refuse.

God offered a covenant containing three promises to Abraham (Genesis 12:1-3):
—a land;
—a great nation (descendants);
—a special relationship to God that will benefit all people.

Abraham accepted the covenant by believing that God would do what God had promised. God did not have to promise anything. Likewise, Abraham might have proceeded to live as if he did not believe God would follow through. Things could have been otherwise. But God offered and Abraham accepted the covenant.

Watch for references to the theme of covenant in the remaining chapters of this book.

Read It for Yourself

Read Genesis 18:1-15.

The Oaks of Mamre [MAM-ree] mentioned in verse 1 apparently refer to a grove of trees that served as a landmark in the general area where Abraham lived at that time. The oaks probably were situated slightly to the north of Hebron [HEE-bruhn]. Hebron was a Canaanite royal city built on a hillside about nineteen miles south of the future site of Jerusalem. Abraham later purchased a cave in the area to serve as a tomb for his family.

From your reading of this passage, who do you think the three men might have been?

Herodian walls surround the caves at Machpelah where Abraham and Sarah are buried.

Neither ancient traditions nor modern scholars agree on how these three men should be identified. Some say that they were really three angels (compare this passage with the statement in Hebrews 13:2). Others say that God and two angels made up the trio. This idea seems to fit, especially when one adds in the references made in Genesis 18:22 and 19:1. Some early Christians saw the three strangers as representing the three persons of the Trinity—God the Father, the Son, and the Holy Spirit. In whatever way we understand this scene, it does appear certain that God was present to and spoke with Abraham on this occasion.

Verses 1-8 display a marvelous example of hospitality. What do you notice when you compare Abraham's statement in verses 4-5 with his actions in verses 6-8?

On the basis of verses 9-15, how would you describe the faith of Abraham and Sarah?

Sometimes God's promises and actions move beyond the human capacity to believe. At such times we are challenged by the question asked in the first part of verse 14. Write that question here.

In his Gospel, Luke contemplates this question twice. Read each account.

Luke 1:26-38 (especially verse 37): The angel Gabriel announces to Mary that she and her elderly relative Elizabeth will give birth to sons.

Luke 18:18-30 (especially verse 27): Jesus responds to the disciples who were worried about who could enter the kingdom of God if a rich person could not. Note what happened soon afterward when a rich man named Zacchaeus [za-KEE-uhs] encountered Jesus (Luke 19:1-9).

What do these passages suggest about the nature of God's promises and human faith?

Let the Bible Form You

Spend some time with Psalm 146. You might want to try using it in a morning prayer time for several days.

Throughout Psalm 146, claims are made about God's faithfulness and justice on the one hand (verses 5-9) and humanity's lack of those qualities on the other (verses 3-4). Moreover, this psalm helps us see that God's faithfulness and human faithfulness are different qualities. God's faithfulness may be described as God's ongoing trustworthiness. Verse 6 expresses this idea well. Yet when human beings find it possible to be faithful, their faithfulness may better be described as a willingness to trust. So it was that God counted Abraham's willingness to trust God's promises as righteousness (Genesis 15:6).

Try this experiment in permitting the words of Psalm 146 to form you inwardly:

- ▶ Ask God in prayer to permit the words of the psalm to work in your life.
- ▶ Read Psalm 146 at least once and preferably more times. Repetition helps the words to work below your conscious level.
- ▶ Take additional time, at least another three minutes, contemplating the fullness of God's faithfulness.
- ▶ Close your eyes and become quiet inside yourself. Let your breathing become a natural rhythm. As you breathe in and out, think the words *Praise God* with the rhythm of your breath.
- ▶ Close by praying the words of the hymn printed below.

I'll praise my Maker while I've breath;
and when my voice is lost in death,
praise shall employ my nobler powers.
My days of praise shall ne'er be past,
while life, and thought, and being last,
or immortality endures.

Happy are they whose hopes rely on
   Israel's God,
who made the sky and earth and seas,
   with all their train;
whose truth forever stands secure,
who saves th' oppressed and feeds the
   poor,
for none shall find God's promise vain.

The Lord pours eyesight on the blind;
the Lord supports the fainting mind and
   sends the
laboring conscience peace.
God helps the stranger in distress,
the widow and the fatherless,
and grants the prisoner sweet release.

I'll praise my God who lends me
   breath;
and when my voice is lost in death,
praise shall employ my nobler powers.
My days of praise shall ne'er be past,
while life, and thought, and being last,
or immortality endures.
—Isaac Watts

CHAPTER 3

GOD
DELIVERS
THE
PEOPLE

In this chapter you will

- identify oppression, as seen in the Egyptian enslavement of the Israelites

- see God's response to oppression

- consider ways to work with God toward deliverance

How Did the Hebrews Get to Egypt?

The time of Abraham and Sarah, around 2100 B.C., and the time of Moses, around 1250 B.C., are separated by about 850 years. The biblical record of that period includes the stories of Isaac, Jacob, and Joseph.

Isaac's stories are found in Genesis 21–28. The stories about Jacob, Isaac's son and twin brother to Esau, are found in Genesis 25–50. Within the Jacob stories are found the stories about his son Joseph, famous for the coat of many colors and for the interpretation of dreams. The stories about Joseph may be found in Genesis 37–50.

Because of envy, Joseph's brothers conspired for him to fall into the hands of some traders, who sold Joseph to Potiphar, one of the high officials in the government of the Egyptian pharaoh (ruler). By God's favor, Joseph rose to the position of prime minister of Egypt, second in power only to pharaoh himself. During a famine, Joseph's brothers migrated to Egypt; and there the Hebrews remained and prospered for several centuries.

Oppression

Oppression involves the use of power by one person or group to force their will upon another person or group. Read Exodus 1:8-14 for an example of oppression.

Why did the Egyptians seek to oppress the Israelites?

According to Genesis 45:10, Joseph and his brothers had settled in Goshen [GOH-shuhn], a rich grazing area in the northeast part of the Nile Delta. Goshen was a border region within Egypt. Exodus 1:9-10 indicates that during an unsettled time of political and military struggle with kingdoms in western Asia, the pharaoh feared the Israelites would be a national security risk. Oppression is often the political structure that fear takes.

Moreover, a new royal family had moved into power within Egypt. The new pharaoh of verse 8, "who did not know Joseph," was probably either Seti I or Rameses [RAM-uh-seez] II. During this period of transition, the capital of the Egyptian empire was moved from Thebes in southern Egypt to the Goshen region in the north. Slaves were used to build the new capital. Verse 11 refers to the building of new administrative centers in the region.

Exodus 1:15–2:10 tells of some ways by which the Hebrews sought to thwart genocidal policies

Statue of Rameses II, pharaoh of Egypt

An Egyptian workman places mudbricks in the sun to dry and harden.

established by the Egyptians. Victims of oppression must find whatever ways they can to outwit their oppressors simply to survive.

These verses also reveal another type of oppression experienced by the Hebrews. Exodus 2:1-2 tells of the birth of a baby who would grow up to become the liberator of God's people. Yet in verse 10, that baby is given the name *Moses*—an Egyptian name for a Hebrew baby.

Because oppressors tend to wish all the world to be shaped by them, they often force their victims to take on names that are to the liking of the oppressors. Many African-Americans are aware of how their ancestors lost their African names when sold into slavery in the United States. White slave owners forced new names, often only first names with a classical Greek or Roman sound, on their slaves. If slaves had any last name, it was usually recorded as the family name of the white slave owner. In recent years some African-Americans have sought to put the trappings of slavery behind them by changing their American "slave" names to African or Muslim names.

What examples of modern oppression are you aware of?

God Keeps God's Promises

God promised Abraham three things: a great nation made up of numerous descendants of Abraham, a special relationship to God that would benefit all people, and a land (Genesis 12:1-3). Even in the midst of their slavery, the fulfillment of God's promises was evident in the lives of the Hebrew people.

A great nation of numerous descendants: Exodus 1:7 best describes the fulfillment of this promise: "But the Israelites were fruitful and prolific; they multiplied and grew exceedingly strong, so that the land was filled with them." Note the several different ways in which the increasing numbers of the Israelites is mentioned in just this one sentence. Also note the irony found in Exodus 1:12: "The more they were oppressed, the more they multiplied and spread, so that the Egyptians came to dread the Israelites."

A special relationship to God, benefiting all people: The Exodus involved other peoples besides the Israelites, according to Exodus 12:37-38. Thus the deliverance from slavery worked by

What's in a Name?

The several different names used to refer to the people of God in the Bible can be confusing. For example, throughout the Book of Exodus, the words *Hebrew* and *Israelite* seem to be used interchangeably. Here is an attempt at making some distinctions:

Hebrews: an ethnic group that migrated from Mesopotamia into Canaan about 2100 B.C. At some point, they also became known as Israelites; and the two terms are synonymous for our purposes. Technically, the Hebrews were

Israelites: the descendants of Eber, great grandson of Shem, son of Noah, according to Genesis 10–11. members of the twelve Hebrew tribes that settled in Canaan following the Exodus from Egypt and the wandering through the wilderness of the Sinai Peninsula. These twelve tribes were said to be descended from the twelve sons of Jacob, who was also known as Israel. Hence, the "children" or descendants of Israel/Jacob were known as Israelites. When the kingdom of Israel divided into two portions in 922 B.C., the Northern Kingdom became known as Israel.

Judeans: the inhabitants of the Southern Kingdom of Judah, following the division of the United Kingdom of Israel. After the Babylonian Exile of 586–538 B.C. and the conquest of the area by Persians and Greeks, this southern region became known as Judea.

Jews: the people of Israel after the Exile. In the New Testament persons might be called Jews by reason of either nationality or religion. Today, the term *Jews* still refers to members either of the ethnic group or the religion.

NOTE: The term *Israeli* should only be used to refer to a citizen or inhabitant of the modern nation-state of Israel, which was founded in A.D. 1948.

God for the Israelites benefited others as well. Note that even Pharaoh, at the depth of his despair, pleaded with Moses and Aaron to ask their God for a blessing on him (Exodus 12:30-32).

The **promise of a land** would have to wait until the conquest of Canaan under Joshua's leadership, following the long period when the Exodus generation of Israelites wandered in the wilderness.

Moses and the Burning Bush

While hiding out from the Egyptians after murdering an Egyptian overseer who was abusing a Hebrew slave, Moses encountered God. God called Moses to lead the Hebrews out of their slavery toward the land God had promised to Abraham. But Moses tried to dodge the responsibility in four ways.

This icon of Moses shows two momentous events in his life: receiving the tablets of the law from God and meeting God at the burning bush.

Exodus 3:11-12 Moses claimed to be a nobody whom the Israelites could never be convinced to follow.

BUT... God said the sign that God had called Moses for this task was that the Israelites would someday worship God at the very place where Moses and God were that moment talking.

Exodus 3:13-14 Moses claimed that the Israelites would want to know more about this God who was promising to free them.

BUT... God said to tell the people that God's name (and perhaps the essential quality of God) is "I AM."

Exodus 4:1-9 Moses feared that the Israelites and the Egyptians would not believe him.

BUT... God said that God would enable Moses to perform a series of marvelous signs to convince any skeptics.

Exodus 4:10-16 Moses claimed not to have the ability to speak well. (Possibly, since Moses was reared in an Egyptian household, his Hebrew might have been heavily accented and hence unacceptable to many Israelites.)

BUT... God provided Moses' brother, Aaron, to take care of the speaking tasks.

The Ten Plagues

To convince Pharaoh to release the Israelites from their slavery, God enabled Moses and Aaron to inflict ten plagues on the Egyptians:

1. The pollution of the Nile River (Exodus 7:14-25)
2. Frogs (Exodus 8:1-15)
3. Gnats (Exodus 8:16-19)
4. Flies (Exodus 8:20-32)
5. Livestock diseased (Exodus 9:1-7)
6. Boils (Exodus 9:8-12)
7. Thunder and hail (Exodus 9:13-35)
8. Locusts (Exodus 10:1-20)
9. Darkness (Exodus 10:21-29)
10. Deaths of the Egyptian first-born males (Exodus 12:29-32)

The Cost of Salvation

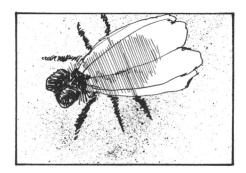

Perhaps the most deeply fundamental belief of Judaism is that God saved the Israelites from slavery in Egypt in the event of the Exodus. God acted within history to deliver God's specially chosen people—the Israelites—from a killing oppression and to lead them into a new land, providing them along the way with sustenance and a way of life.

All these elements together make up a biblical understanding of salvation. Salvation is not just relief from a horribly bad existence and the reality of impending death. Salvation also involves the giving of gifts: life itself and a healthy, fulfilling way to live. The salvation begun in leaving slavery behind in Egypt is not complete without the giving of the law at Mount Sinai.

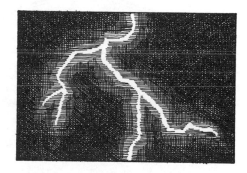

In addition, in the Exodus story, salvation is an utterly serious and costly matter. A real price is paid for the salvation of the Israelites. Blood—understood in the Old Testament as the essence of life itself—is spilled. Blood is shed for the sake of the salvation of the Israelites in three ways:

—An unblemished lamb is slaughtered by each Israelite household and its blood sprinkled on the door frame of the house as a sign that the tenth plague of the slaughter of the first-born males is to "pass over" and not attack the Israelites within (Exodus 12:1-13).

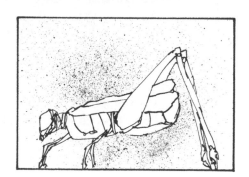

—The first-born males of the Egyptians—humans and animals alike, and even the first-born son of Pharaoh—die in the tenth plague. The terrible anguish suffered by the Egyptians convinces Pharaoh, at least momentarily, to let the Israelites leave Egypt (Exodus 12:29-32).

—The soldiers of the Egyptian army are drowned in vast numbers when the waters of the sea return after parting for the passage of the Israelites during their escape from Egypt (Exodus 14:26-31).

Read It for Yourself

The Book of Exodus tells the stories of two of the most significant events in the history of Jews and Christians: the salvation of the Israelites from slavery in Egypt and the giving of the covenant laws at Mount Sinai in the desert. Jews and Christians see God acting in special ways in these events, shaping their understandings of themselves as God's people.

Read Exodus 19:1-9. This passage tells of the beginnings of the preparations for Moses and Aaron to see and hear God on behalf of the people of Israel as they camp at Mount Sinai. All the

The Ten Commandments

God's Exclusive Claims
1. No Other Gods (Exodus 20:2-3)
2. No Image of God (Exodus 20:4-6)
3. No Misuse of God's Power (Exodus 20:7)

God's Basic Institutions
4. No Work on the Seventh Day (Exodus 20:8-11)
5. No Contempt for the Family (Exodus 20:12)

Basic Human Obligations
6. No Contempt for Human Life (Exodus 20:13)
7. No Contempt for Sex (Exodus 20:14)

Basic Social Obligations
8. No Contempt for the Goods of the Community (Exodus 20:15)
9. No Contempt for the Community's Institutions (Exodus 20:16)
10. No Lusting After the Life or Goods of Others (Exodus 20:17)

Based on the grouping and summary of the commandments found throughout *The Ten Commandments and Human Rights*, by Walter Harrelson; Fortress Press, 1980.

events detailed in Exodus 19–40, in the entire Book of Leviticus, and in Numbers 1:1–10:10 took place at Mount Sinai during an eleven-month encampment.

Focus on Exodus 19:3-6. With what three phrases does God describe God's intentions for the Israelites?

What do the Israelites have to do in order to be God's special people?

Read 1 Peter 2:9 and compare it with Exodus 19:3-6. The first generations of Christians understood the covenant relationship first made by God with the Israelites in the time of the Exodus to apply to them in their time. In what ways do these phrases describing God's intentions for God's people apply to you?

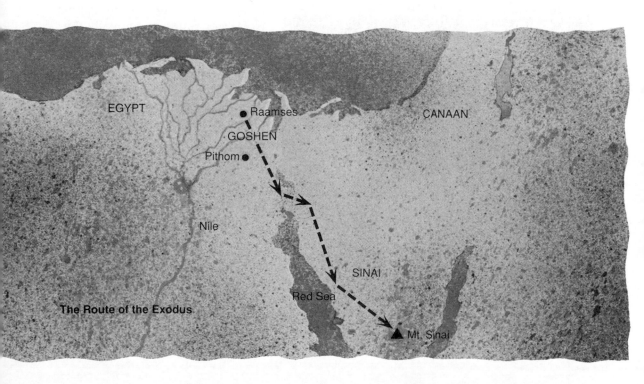

EGYPT

Raamses

GOSHEN

Pithom

CANAAN

Nile

SINAI

Red Sea

The Route of the Exodus

Mt. Sinai

Let the Bible Form You

Instead of starting with the Bible for spiritual formation, spend some time reading your daily newspaper. Make a list of the news stories about victims of oppression of various types and about struggle for liberation. At this point, suspend any judgment about the morality of apparent oppressors or victims.

Now read Psalm 137 aloud or silently. What emotions did you feel as you read this psalm?

What emotions did you sense the writer of the psalm expressing?

The Israelites hung up their musical instruments in Babylonia; they could not sing the Lord's song in a foreign land (Psalm 137).

By way of information, Psalm 137 is a prayer for vengeance against Israel's enemies, specifically the Babylonians and their allies the Edomites, who destroyed Jerusalem and the Temple in 587–586 B.C. You will read more about this tragedy in in the next chapter.

The Israelites knew the Temple as God's special dwelling place. It was their central place for worship. When the Babylonians and the Edomites tore down the Temple, they not only robbed the Israelites of a crucial part of their religion, they also insulted God.

The psalmist was among the Israelite hostages taken into exile in Babylonia. He had seen the Temple destroyed. His way of life had been obliterated. All hope had been torn away. Now his conquerors wanted him to trivialize and profane his relig-

Haitians, trying to escape to the United States, crowd aboard a boat.

ion further by singing the sacred songs of worship for their entertainment value.

At first reading, we might be surprised, shocked, and embarrassed by the raw emotion expressed in this psalm, especially in the gruesome wish of verse 9. How can we justify such bloodthirstiness in Holy Scripture?

Psalm 137's deep honesty justifies itself. The writer openly shares with God his deepest and most painful feelings of despair, hatred, rage, and desire for revenge. The writer holds nothing back from God.

Pause now and visualize one of the victims of the oppressive situations about which you read in your newspaper. Imagine yourself in that victim's place. Read Psalm 137 again, and yet one more time. Can you begin to understand what Psalm 137 expresses?

Spend a moment in prayer asking God what God's will is for you, given the situations of oppression around you this day.

This chapter has no psalm response, for "how could we sing the LORD's song in a foreign land?" What song can we sing when humans inflict suffering on other humans all around us?

CHAPTER 4

GOD
JUDGES
AND
RESTORES
THE
PEOPLE

In this chapter you will

- learn about the prophets

- diagnose the problem of human disobedience

- ponder alternative ways of living and their consequences

- look to God for help

How Did God's People Get to Babylonia?

Centuries passed between the time of Moses and the time of the prophets discussed in this chapter. Many significant events occurred, and fascinating persons lived during those years. You might wish to read about that period in the books of Joshua, Judges, Ruth, First and Second Samuel, and First and Second Kings.

For now, a timetable will help you fill in the gaps between the time of Moses and the persons and events covered in this chapter.

APPROX. 1250 B.C.	Moses leads the Israelites out of slavery in Egypt.
APPROX. 1200–1020	The Israelites fight wars to conquer Canaan and are ruled by judges.
APPROX. 1020–1000	Saul reigns as the first king of Israel.
APPROX. 1005–961	David reigns as the second king of Israel and establishes Jerusalem as the capital.
961–928	Solomon reigns as the third king of Israel and builds the Temple in Jerusalem.
922	After the death of Solomon, the kingdom is divided into the Northern Kingdom of Israel (with its capital at Samaria) and the Southern Kingdom of Judah (with its capital at Jerusalem).
APPROX. 850	The prophet Elijah is active during the reign of King Ahab of Israel.
755–725	The prophet Hosea is active during the reign of King Jeroboam II of Israel and during the following period of political crisis.
722–721	The Northern Kingdom of Israel is conquered by the Assyrian Empire.
626–587	The prophet Jeremiah is active during the reign of King Josiah of Judah and during the following period of political crisis.
587–586	The Southern Kingdom of Judah is conquered by the Babylonian Empire; the Jerusalem Temple is destroyed.
586–538	The Babylonian Exile
539	Babylonia is conquered by the Persian Empire.
538	Emperor Cyrus of Persia proclaims that the Judeans may return to their homeland.
520–515	Zerubbabel leads the effort to rebuild the Jerusalem Temple.
445	Nehemiah is appointed the governor of Judea by the Persian emperor.
427–397	Ezra is active in Judea.

What's in a Name?

Have you ever found the Bible hard to read aloud because of those unpronounceable names? You may have noticed the pronunciation guides for some of the names in earlier chapters. Perhaps your Bible also includes marks that will help you with pronunciation.

Here is a guide for pronouncing some of the names you will encounter in this chapter.

Carchemish [KAHR-kuh-mish]

Gomer [GOH-muhr]

Hosea [hoh-ZAY-uh]

Jehoiakim [ji-HOI-uh-kim]

Jeroboam [jer-hu-BOH-uhm]

Josiah [joh-SI-uh]

Megiddo [mi-GID-oh]

Nebuchadnezzar [neb-uh-kuhd-NEZ-uhr]

Nehemiah [nee-huh-MI-uh]

Sennacherib [suh-NAK-uh-rib]

Zedekiah [zed-uh-KI-uh]

Zerubbabel [zuh-RUHB-uh-buhl]

A Persian king on his throne

What Is a Prophet?

The short answer is that a prophet is someone who speaks the word God wants shared with the people. The popular image of a prophet as someone who predicts the future is not completely accurate. A prophet is not a fortune teller, peering into a crystal ball or reading entrails, trying to perceive the particulars of what is about to happen.

However, a prophet does read the "signs of the times." The Old Testament prophets knew what was happening culturally and politically around them. Combining that awareness with an acute sensitivity to the will of God, the prophets often were able to say that if the people continued to live in the way they currently were, then such-and-such would happen.

The key to understanding the prophets is this sensitivity to the will of God. More than simply sharp observers of the life of their nations, the prophets were persons to whom God granted the ability to discern God's will for their time and place.

Mostly, the prophets called their people back from various forms of idolatry and immorality, warned them about God's judgment and the consequences of continuing in their behavior, and offered God's amazing words of comfort when dire consequences did befall them.

For example, for most of his time as a prophet,

Jeremiah warned his people of the consequences of their unfaithfulness. He urged them to accept the unacceptable advice of surrendering to the Babylonian army rather than placing their faith in military forces and alliances. Once, however, the Babylonian siege against Jerusalem showed the hopelessness of the Judean situation, Jeremiah began talking about the hope God offered beyond the present situation.

The Prophet Hosea and His Times

Hosea became active as a prophet in the Northern Kingdom of Israel toward the end of the reign of King Jeroboam II. Jeroboam's forty years as king were a relatively lengthy, stable, and prosperous period. During that time, however, the Israelites became overly satisfied with themselves. Things were easy, they thought; and so things would always be easy. However, after the death of Jeroboam, Israel's situation began to fall apart.

Israel found itself to be a rather minor nation caught between two superpowers—Egypt and Assyria. Israel wavered in its alliances, first with one, then with the other, while wanting to be swallowed up by neither. During this time also, Israel suffered severe internal political crises. Second Kings 15–17 records a steady series of royal assassinations and revolts. Although Jeroboam had reigned forty years, the next twenty-five years saw six different kings. Four of those six kings were murdered; the sixth king was captured and imprisoned by the Assyrians.

Hosea's book tells of God's anguish at the unfaithfulness of the people of Israel and calls on the people to return to God. Much of Hosea's message is acted out in his home life, as God calls on Hosea to continue to love his unfaithful wife, Gomer.

Read Hosea 3 for a taste of Hosea's message. On one level, Hosea either buys his wife from prostitution or pays her lover to return her. Hosea then sets up a period of probation for Gomer in their household, expecting her best behavior. On the national level, the Israelites have lived in their relationship to God as if they were Hosea's wife. They have turned to pagan gods and rituals. But God has sought to buy them back from their idolatry, even though that redemption is costly. Israel, also, will undergo a period of probation, a time without a national or religious life; but ultimately Israel will be restored to a good relationship with God.

Hosea and Gomer

An Indictment

Based on the testimony of the prophet Hosea (Hosea 4:1-3), God brings suit against the people on the following charges:

—Unfaithfulness
—Disloyalty
—Refusal to acknowledge any relationship with God
—Swearing
—Lying
—Murder
—Theft
—Adultery
—Crimes against the environment

How do the people plead?

(Not guilty? Guilty?)

"Your ways and your doings have brought this upon you. This is your doom; how bitter it is! It has reached your very heart."

(Jeremiah 4:18)

Jeremiah lamenting the destruction of Jerusalem

The Prophet Jeremiah and His Times

Although Hosea and Jeremiah lived over a century apart in time and in different kingdoms, their basic messages were similar. Like Hosea, Jeremiah sought to call his people to a faithful and obedient relationship with God.

For forty years, Jeremiah warned Judah of the judgment and destructive punishment to come if the people did not set their lives in order in relation to God. His message was difficult for the people to swallow. In fact, on one occasion Jeremiah was arrested for treason (Jeremiah 37:11-21). On another occasion, an attempt was made to kill him (Jeremiah 38:1-13).

The tone of Jeremiah's message was uncompromising.

The people and leaders of Judah felt confident that the devastation that befell the Northern Kingdom of Israel over a century earlier could not happen to them. In 701 B.C., they survived a scare when King Sennacherib of Assyria attempted to invade them. Although Judah continued to exist for a while longer, primarily because it was a relatively unimportant pawn in the games of the superpowers, its people held on firmly to the conviction that God would faithfully preserve the nation and king of Judah. Judah's religious leaders found Jeremiah's message to be dangerously deviant.

Judah did show some hope of reforming morally and religiously under King Josiah's leadership, starting in 621. But Josiah was killed in a battle with the Egyptians at Megiddo in 609. Josiah's successors failed to carry forth his efforts.

Also in 609, the Assyrian Empire fell to a new rising world power, Babylonia. In 605, Babylonia defeated the other major power, Egypt, in a battle against its main army at Carchemish. Then Babylonia demanded tribute from the smaller nations of the region, including Judah. In 601, King Jehoiakim of Judah attempted to rebel. In 597, a Babylonian army put down the Judean rebellion and deported many leading citizens to Babylonia. Then in 589, King Zedekiah attempted yet another rebellion. This time, rebellion brought complete ruin as Nebuchadnezzar's army tore down Jerusalem's walls, pillaged the city, destroyed the Temple, took massive numbers of Judeans to Babylonia, and for the most part destroyed Judah as a nation.

Read Jeremiah 8:4-12 for another sample of Jeremiah's message to his people. Verses 4-7 wonder why the people are so morally indifferent despite the fact that their disobedience goes against their own self-interest. Verses 8-9 contrast the law of the Lord as interpreted by the religious leaders and scholars with the real word of the Lord as spoken through Jeremiah. Verse 10 warns about the consequences of gross injustice in the land. Verses 11-12 condemn the easy answers offered by the religious leaders and accepted by the people.

Choosing Death Instead of Life

Second Kings 24:8–25:12 describes the fall of Jerusalem and Judah. The causes of the destruction, however, existed long before the events described occurred. Those causes had little to do with either military weakness or diplomatic failures.

In Deuteronomy 30:15-20, Moses challenges the Israelites to choose between the way that leads to life and the way that leads to death. He calls on them to make their choice before they enter the promised land of Canaan.

Israel said "life" that day; but in the long run, it chose death. The curses stated in Deuteronomy 28:15-68 came to pass with Judah's defeat at the hands of the Babylonians. As threatened in Deuteronomy 28:68, the exodus from slavery had been undone. The covenant promise was broken, not by God, but by Israel's actions.

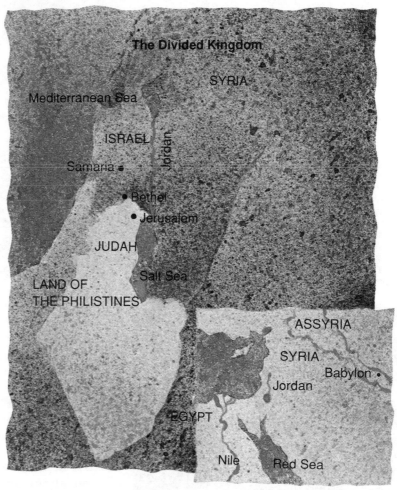

The Divided Kingdom

The Trauma of the Exile

What could be more terrible than seeing your homeland overrun by an invader, seeing the center of your religious life torn down and profaned, seeing everything that gave your nation its identity erased from existence, and being taken yourself to the other side of the world as a captive to serve the needs of the invaders?

That is what the Exile in Babylonia meant to a

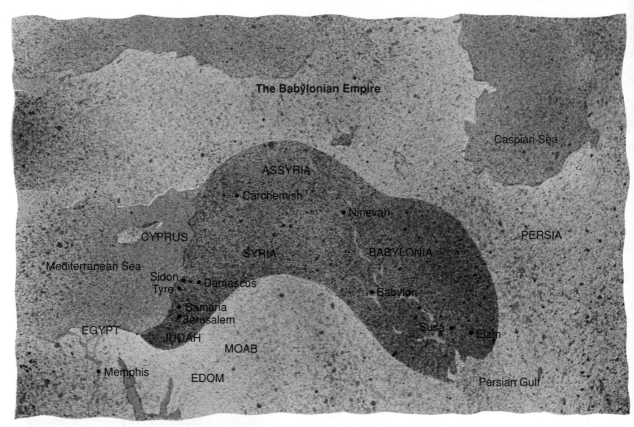

The Babylonian Empire

Caspian Sea

ASSYRIA

• Carchemish

• Ninevah

CYPRUS

PERSIA

Mediterranean Sea

SYRIA

BABYLONIA

Sidon
Tyre • • Damascus

• Babylon

• Samaria
• Jerusalem

EGYPT

JUDAH

Susa •

• Elam

MOAB

• Memphis

EDOM

Persian Gulf

Judean exiles carrying their possessions

Judean. Most persons reading this book have never experienced a tragedy of that magnitude. Perhaps only three other events in the history of the Jewish people can be considered as horrible as the Exile: slavery in Egypt before Moses led the Exodus in 1250 B.C., the second destruction of Jerusalem and the Temple by the Romans in A.D. 70, and the Holocaust at the hands of the Nazis in the 1930's and 1940's.

Return of the Exiles

Jeremiah predicted an exile period of seventy years (Jeremiah 29:10). In reality, the time between the destruction of the Temple in 587 B.C. and its complete restoration in 515 was a period of seventy-two years. For the Jews, the crucial point was that their exile did not last forever. God acted to bring their exile to an end.

As the Jews saw things, God had raised up Nebuchadnezzar and the Babylonians to their position of world power in order to judge and punish the Jews for their unfaithful disobedience to the covenant. Likewise, they believed that God raised up King Cyrus of Persia to conquer the Babylonians and to restore the Jews to their homeland.

The different approaches of the two empires to dealing with conquered nations served the purposes God had at different times. The Babylonians sought security by uprooting peoples and tearing down their cultures. The Persians sought stability by offering peoples some power to determine their

The Cyrus Cylinder commemorates Cyrus's restoration works after he captured Babylonia.

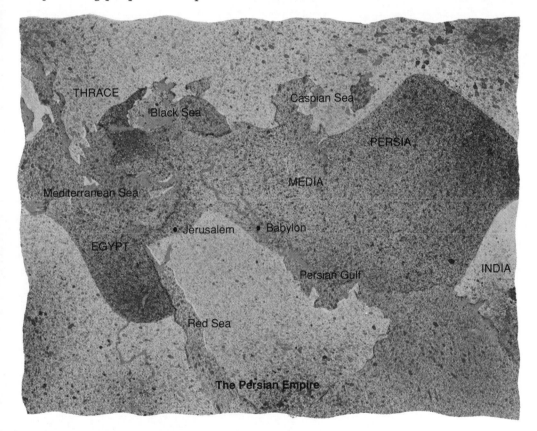

The Persian Empire

own lives and to preserve their own distinct cultures and religions.

So it was that in 538 B.C., Cyrus proclaimed the decree found in Ezra 1:2-4. Not only was it important that the decree permitted the Jews to return to Judea, but further significance was found in the fact that it was the Lord who "stirred up the spirit of King Cyrus of Persia" (Ezra 1:1) to bring about this great event.

Read It for Yourself

Read Jeremiah 31:31-34.

Think about what was going on when Jeremiah uttered these words at the urging of God. Probably this passage was spoken to the people of Judah just before Jerusalem fell in 587 B.C. Review the section on "The Prophet Jeremiah and His Times," and describe briefly what was going on.

Recall what you have read so far about the word *covenant*. You might find it helpful to read Deuteronomy 6:1-9.

Through Jeremiah, God announced the making of a new covenant (Jeremiah 31:31). What makes this covenant "new"?

In what ways is the "new" covenant like the "old" covenant?

What does this passage about the new covenant tell you about God?

What does this passage tell you about humanity?

Let the Bible Form You

Throughout this book, you have been using psalms for spiritual formation. In the form in which we have them today, the psalms were probably gathered and edited for use within the Second

Temple—the Temple rebuilt by Zerubbabel after the Exile. Thus there is a sense in which we share in the worship experience of the restored people of Israel whenever we use psalms to worship God and to nurture our spirits.

Quiet down inside even if there is noise around you on the outside. Then read Psalm 130 silently or aloud.

We cannot say with certainty when this psalm was written, nor for what occasion. However, we might imagine the restored people of God gathering to confess their sins, to meditate on the new covenant God had written in their hearts, and to express gratitude to God for God's mercy.

Verses 3-6 indicate that it is in God's very nature to be merciful, even to those who sin against God. Therefore, the psalmist feels confident in trusting God, even given the psalmist's own sinful imperfection.

Verses 7-8 suggest that the entire people should likewise trust God in their difficulties.

Read Psalm 130 again. Close your eyes, and imagine a voice welling up from deep within your body. That voice cries out to God. What does the voice say?

Offer to God whatever that deep-seated voice says.

Now, imagine yourself sitting in the night, facing a window and looking at the darkness outside. You are watching for the coming of morning. What do you see? How do you wait? Is it difficult to wait?

Then imagine the Lord coming and accepting what that voice deep within you has cried out.

Read Psalm 130 one more time.

Conclude by singing or humming the psalm response printed below.

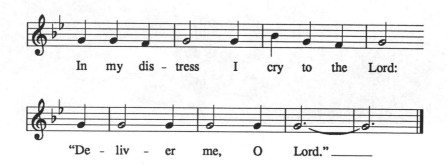

In my dis-tress I cry to the Lord:
"De-liv-er me, O Lord." _____

CHAPTER 5

GOD
COMES
TO THE
PEOPLE

In this chapter you will

- look at what the Bible claims about Jesus

- consider what Jesus shows us about God

- explore what you believe about Jesus

New Testament Times

Although no one can say for sure when New Testament events happened, one informed guess looks like this.

4 B.C. Jesus is born.

A.D. 27 Jesus begins his public ministry.

30 Jesus is crucified and resurrected.

33 Paul is converted to faith in Christ.

50 Paul writes his first letter: First Thessalonians.

60 Paul dies in Rome.

70 Jerusalem is destroyed by the Romans; Mark's Gospel is written.

85 Matthew's and Luke's Gospels are written.

100 John's Gospel is written.

While Jesus Lived

. . . the Roman Empire surrounded the entire Mediterranean Sea.

. . . Galilee and Judea were ruled by the Romans.

. . . the Great Wall of China had already been built.

The Great Wall of China

. . . the Mayan civilization was developing in Central America.

. . . Buddhism was already five hundred years old in India.

. . . Tiberius succeeded Augustus as Roman emperor.

Statue of Buddha in Kyoto, Japan

. . . there were two hundred million people throughout the entire world.

Roman coin of Emperor Tiberius

What's in a Name?

The Gospel writers use many different names for Jesus. These names reveal a wide variety of understandings of who Jesus is and what he was sent to do.

What do the following passages say about the meaning of these names?

Messiah/Christ —Matthew 16:13-26
Son of Man —Matthew 25:31-46
Teacher/Rabbi —Luke 10:25-37
Son of God —John 3:16-21
Savior —John 4
Good Shepherd —John 10:1-18

Who do you say that Jesus is?

What Did Jesus Do?

The four Gospels—Matthew, Mark, Luke, and John—provide us with our only accounts of what Jesus did and taught during his ministry. However, these evangelists were not concerned with writing Jesus' biography. We cannot merge the four Gospels into one straightforward account of Jesus' life. The Gospels are too different in their viewpoints and in their reporting of the sequence of events.

However, we know that in the fullness of his adulthood (Luke tells us Jesus was about thirty years old), Jesus began to preach throughout Galilee and Judea. Mark provides us with a summary of Jesus' message: "The time is fulfilled, and the kingdom of God has come near; repent, and believe in the good news" (Mark 1:15).

We know that Jesus went around Galilee **teaching**. The most famous example of Jesus' teachings is the Sermon on the Mount, found in Matthew 5–7. Jesus also taught using parables, pithy stories relating everyday experiences to the kingdom of God. One of the best known, the parable of the good Samaritan, is found in Luke 10:25-37.

We know that Jesus also went about **healing**. For example, in Matthew 8:1-17, Jesus heals a leper, the servant of a Roman centurion, and Peter's mother-in-law. These healings were not significant as supernatural miracles; rather, they were important because they pointed to what God's kingdom is like.

We know that Jesus suffered **crucifixion**—that he was hanged from a cross after being found guilty of anti-Roman activities. The long accounts in the Gospels of Jesus' Passion—the events leading up to his death—include the stories about the Last Supper, Jesus' prayer in the garden of Gethsemane, his betrayal by Judas and arrest by the Jewish authorities, his trials before the Jewish and Roman leaders, his torture, and finally his death on the cross.

But we also know that Jesus experienced **resurrection**. We have no idea exactly what happened when God raised Jesus from death. But we have the testimonies in the Gospels that something happened. Jesus' tomb was found empty, and Jesus appeared to several of his disciples. Oddly, the Gospels disagree about most of the details of the resurrection appearances. However, they uniformly agree that Jesus was resurrected.

Who Is Jesus?

The writers of the Gospels were primarily interested in persuading persons to believe that Jesus is the Messiah. *Messiah* and *Christ* mean the same thing: "the Anointed One." *Christ* is the Greek version of the Hebrew word *Messiah*. Strictly speaking, neither is part of Jesus' name. Sometimes we get so used to saying "Jesus Christ" together that we think of "Christ" as Jesus' last name. However, "Christ" is a title. To say "Jesus Christ" is to proclaim that Jesus is the "Anointed One of God." Or, if we look at the history of the idea of the Messiah, we will find that we are really saying "Jesus, King" when we use the phrase Jesus Christ.

A time came in Israel's history when the Philistines threatened its survival (about 1020 B.C.). At that time, God told the prophet Samuel to anoint a king. First Samuel 9:27–10:1 tells how the prophet Samuel anointed Saul's head with oil as a sign of setting Saul apart to be king over Israel. First Samuel 16:13 tells of Samuel later anointing David king. We are further told that with that anointing, "the spirit of the LORD came mightily upon David from that day forward."

Literally, Saul and David, as well as later kings of Israel and Judah, were "anointed ones"—messiahs. However, in later troubled times in Israel's history, a different understanding of messiah arose.

According to 2 Samuel 7, God promised King David that his descendants would sit on his throne forever. When Israel's identity as an independent kingdom was being destroyed by one conquering empire after another, many Jews looked for God to send a messiah—a king like David who would restore Israel to its former greatness. Some of the writings of the prophets were understood as looking for or announcing the coming of such a messiah (for example, Isaiah 9:2-7).

In Jesus' time many Jews looked for God to send a revolutionary leader who would rid them of their Roman rulers. Some of these Jews looked for an ordinary military and political leader. Others, though, looked for a leader to usher in the final kingdom of God at the same time as throwing out the Romans. Yet others, such as the Pharisees, looked for a new, true community in a world to come and saw a revolutionary messiah as a problem rather than as a solution.

One of the basic claims the early Christians made about Jesus was that Jesus is the Messiah, the Christ, the Anointed One. However, they claimed Jesus as still a different sort of messiah. Because Jesus was in fact executed by the Romans as a political threat to their power, the early Christian writings stressed that Jesus never sought to be a revolutionary messiah threatening Roman power. Instead, Jesus reinterpreted the idea of messiah in line with such prophetic texts as Isaiah 52:13–53:12.

These texts looked toward a messiah who was rejected, humiliated, and subjected to suffering and death in order to heal the brokenness of the people. This kind of messiah was quite different from the military leader many Jews expected.

Christians proclaim Jesus as the Messiah God sent in order to free all people from the brokenness and death of their sins. The "kingdom" over which Messiah Jesus rules is not a restored Israel like that of King David. Rather, Jesus' kingdom is the kingdom of heaven itself.

What Does Jesus Show Us About God?

The New Testament makes many claims about who Jesus is, what he has done, and what he shows us about God. One of the most majestic summaries of the early church's beliefs about Jesus is found in Hebrews 1:1-4.

The Letter to the Hebrews shows Jesus as the latest and best revelation of God to humanity. Verses 1-2 set up a series of contrasts:

long ago—in these last days (now)
God spoke to our ancestors—God has spoken to us by the prophets—by a Son

God has come to God's people immediately and intimately in Jesus.

Verses 2-4 tell us several things about the Son. He is

—the heir of all things;
—the force bringing about creation;
—the reflection of God's glory;
—the exact imprint of God's very being;
—the sustainer of all things;
—a priest who makes purification for sins (who offers the sacrifice that cleans away all guilt);
—a prince who occupies the seat of authority at the right hand of God;
—a being much superior to angels. (The Jews of Jesus' time believed angels served to bridge the immeasurable gap between God and humanity. To say Jesus is superior to the angels means that he bridges that gap better.)

Jesus shows us perfectly what God is like and what God intends.

Looking for Proof

We live in a time that demands proof. Before we accept that a fact is true, we want to test it. We tend to be like the stereotype of a Missouri citizen who says, "Show me."

One author has listed six ways people arrive at knowledge:
—by authority (accepting someone else's word);
—by logic (the use of reason);
—by sense experience (what we observe);
—by feelings (emotions, including group loyalty);
—by intuition (insight);
—by scientific experimentation (testing a theory under controlled conditions).
(From *A Question of Values: Six Ways We Make the Personal Choices That Shape Our Lives*, by Hunter Lewis; Harper & Row, Publishers, 1990; pages 10-11.)

According to Matthew 11:2-6, John the Baptist, who was in prison, heard reports about what Jesus was doing in Galilee. John wondered whether Jesus could really be the Messiah. To find out, John sent some of his disciples to Jesus, asking for proof that Jesus was, in fact, the Messiah: "Are you the one who is to come, or are we to wait for another?" (Matthew 11:3).

Jesus provided proof by indicating what was happening because of him:
—the blind receive their sight
—the lame walk
—the lepers are cleansed
—the deaf hear
—the dead are raised

Belief

—More than agreeing that a statement is true
—More than wishing something were true
—From an Old English word meaning "to hold dear," "to desire," "to love," "to trust"
—"For God so loved the world that he gave his only Son, so that everyone who believes in him may not perish but may have eternal life." (John 3:16)

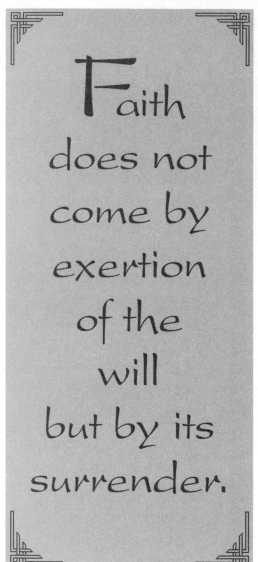

Faith does not come by exertion of the will but by its surrender.

—the poor have good news brought to them

Jesus, John, and John's disciples all knew that these things had been prophesied to occur when God restored God's people from their suffering. Old Testament texts such as Isaiah 29:18-19; 35:5-6a; and 61:1-3 looked forward to a time of peace and health for all God's people. In Luke's Gospel, Jesus begins his ministry by reading from Isaiah 61 in the synagogue in Nazareth and by announcing the fulfillment of that prophecy in himself (4:16-21). The proof of the Messiah, Jesus seemed to say, is in the new creation of wholeness in human lives.

We are never told whether John or his disciples accepted this proof.

What would be enough proof for you to believe that Jesus is the Messiah?

One Man's Struggle to Believe

In May of 1738, John Wesley was thirty-four years old. Although ordained a priest in the Church of England, Wesley found it hard to believe in Christ. After escaping back to London from a failed ministry in the new American colony of Georgia, John filled his journal with entries such as "I knew not that I was *wholly void of this faith* but only thought *I had not enough* of it" and "I well saw no one could . . . have such a sense of forgiveness and not *feel* it. But I felt it not" (from *John Wesley*, edited by Albert C. Outler; Oxford University Press, 1964; pages 64 and 65).

Then John wrote this journal entry for May 24, 1738:

"In the evening, I went very unwillingly to a [Moravian] society [meeting] in Aldersgate Street, where one was reading Luther's Preface to the Epistle to the Romans. About a quarter before nine, while he was describing the change which God works in the heart through faith in Christ, I felt my heart strangely warmed. I felt I did trust in Christ, Christ alone for salvation; and an assurance was given me that he had taken away *my* sins, even *mine*, and saved *me* from the law of sin and death" (from *John Wesley*, page 66).

Though this was not John Wesley's last crisis of faith, he went on to found the spiritual renewal movement known as Methodism. He preached to others what he found to be true in his own life, that believing is accepting that, in Jesus, God has forgiven our sins.

Read It for Yourself

One Gospel text tells better than any other the struggle of the first disciples to understand who Jesus was. Without pausing to take notes or to ask questions, read Matthew 16:13-26.

Write one to three sentences summarizing this passage.

Read the passage again, this time making note of words about which you would like more information. If such resources are available to you, look these words up in a Bible dictionary, concordance, or commentary.

Here are some questions you might want to explore in order to deepen your understanding of this passage:

—To whom or what does the phrase *the Son of man* refer? (verse 13; see Matthew 16:27-28)

—Why would people think that Jesus was John the Baptist? Elijah? Jeremiah? one of the prophets? (verse 14; see Mark 1:14-15; Malachi 4:5-6; as a great prophet, Jesus was naturally compared to other prophets, including Jeremiah)

—What word play does Jesus engage in when he calls Peter a "rock"? (verse 18; see footnotes on this verse in the New Revised Standard Version of the Bible)

—What are "the keys of the kingdom of heaven"? (verse 19; see Acts 10:34-48 for an example of Peter's authority)

—Why might Jesus have called Peter "Satan"? (verse 23; see Matthew 4:1-11)

—What does this passage teach about Jesus' understanding of who he and his disciples are to be? (verses 24-26)

What the Church Believes About Jesus

I believe . . . in Jesus Christ, [God's] only Son our Lord:
 who was conceived by the Holy Spirit,
  born of the Virgin Mary,
  suffered under Pontius Pilate,
  was crucified, dead, and buried;
  [he descended into hell;]
 the third day he rose from the dead;
 he ascended into heaven,
  and sitteth at the right hand of God the Father Almighty;
 from thence he shall come to judge the quick and the dead.

From "The Apostles' Creed, Traditional Version," *The United Methodist Hymnal.*

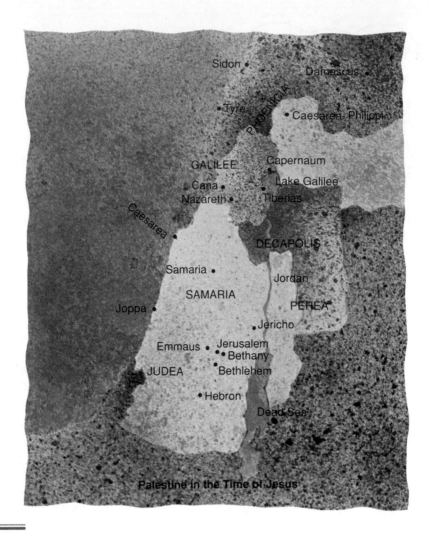

Sidon

Damascus

Tyre
PHOENICIA
Caesarea Philippi

GALILEE
Capernaum
Cana
Lake Galilee
Nazareth
Tiberias

Caesarea

DECAPOLIS

Samaria

Jordan

SAMARIA

PEREA

Joppa

Jericho

Emmaus
Jerusalem
Bethany

JUDEA
Bethlehem

Hebron

Dead Sea

Palestine in the Time of Jesus

If you desired Jesus above all else, what would be different about your life?

Let the Bible Form You

You have a lot of information about Jesus now. How will you let it form you?

Will you move beyond deciding whether to agree that something is factual about Jesus? Will you move beyond whether you have enough proof to accept some statement about Jesus? Will you move toward *desiring* Jesus, *holding* Jesus *dear*, *loving* Jesus, *trusting* Jesus?

Read Psalm 24. One of the main images of this psalm is of the gates and doors of the Temple in Jerusalem. One can visualize the ancient Jews singing this psalm while opening the doors of the Temple to the presence of God, the King of glory.

During the coming week, try for a few minutes

each day to permit Psalm 24 to form your inner spirit. Whether you set aside a special devotional time alone each morning or evening or simply close your eyes and pray for a few moments while commuting on a crowded bus is unimportant. Just take the time to open yourself to the action of God's Spirit within you through the words of Scripture.

Use these suggestions to get started:

▶ Pause and ask God to allow the words of Scripture to work within you.

▶ Read Psalm 24 aloud or silently.

▶ Close your eyes. Let the phrases and images you remember from Psalm 24 paint a picture in your mind.

▶ Perhaps you will imagine a wall. The wall is whatever keeps you from believing in Jesus fully, desiring Jesus. Name that wall. Now imagine a gate in that wall. Is the gate open or shut? If the gate is open, imagine the celebration of the King's entry through it. If the gate is closed, imagine yourself trying to open it. Do you succeed? What needs to happen for the gate to open? Try asking the King to help push the gate open.

▶ Or let the images painted by Psalm 24 take you where they will. Sometimes God's Spirit speaks in ways we never expected.

▶ When you are ready, pray the prayer printed below.

An Invitation to Christ

Come, my Light, and illumine my darkness.
Come, my Life, and revive me from death.
Come, my Physician, and heal my wounds.
Come, Flame of divine love, and burn up the
     thorns of my sins,
  kindling my heart with the flame of thy love.
Come, my King, sit upon the throne of my
     heart and reign there.
For thou alone art my King and my Lord.
Amen.

—Dimitri of Rostov, Russia, 17th century

(From *The Orthodox Way*, by Kallistos Ware; A. R. Mowbray & Co., Ltd.; 1979)

CHAPTER 6

GOD
CALLS
A
NEW
PEOPLE

In this chapter you will

- look at the beginning of the church at the first Christian Pentecost

- consider what the presence and gifts of the Holy Spirit mean for Christians

- explore conversion and the Christian life

- consider your own place within the church

The Acts of the Apostles

Find the Book of the Acts of the Apostles in the New Testament of your Bible. If there is an introduction section to this book, take the time to read it now.

The Acts of the Apostles was written by the same person who wrote the Gospel According to Luke (Luke 1:3; Acts 1:1). Neither book names its author, although the tradition of the church has long been that Luke, a physician who accompanied Paul on some of his missionary travels, wrote both (Colossians 4:14; 2 Timothy 4:11).

The writer of Acts intends to inform Theophilus [thih-AHF-ih-luhs] about the origins of the Christian movement from the days immediately following Jesus' resurrection through the apostle Paul's arrival in Rome. The writer likely wanted Theophilus to look favorably on Christianity. Theophilus was probably a well-placed Roman official. Even if Theophilus would not convert to Christianity, it would be helpful to the Christian movement to recruit Theophilus as a benefactor.

Jewish Pentecost and Christian Pentecost

In Luke's telling of the story of Jesus, at the time following the Resurrection when Jesus disappears from among the disciples (the Ascension), he tells them to remain in Jerusalem until they receive the Holy Spirit (Luke 24:44-53 and Acts 1:6-11). Obedient to Jesus' command, the disciples were present together on the day of the Feast of Pentecost (Acts 2:1).

Jewish tradition holds that seven weeks after the first Passover—when God freed the Israelites from slavery through the plague of the death of the first-born males of the Egyptians (Exodus 12)—God gave the law to Moses and the people at Mount Sinai. In order to remember and celebrate this great event, a festival is held each year. Leviticus 23:15-21 prescribes how Jews are to keep this special day.

Over time, this special celebration came to be known by two names. Because the Jews were to count seven weeks after the Passover, the celebration of the giving of the law became known as the Festival of Weeks. But also because the Jews were to count until the day after the seventh sabbath following Passover—that is until the fiftieth day— the celebration became known by the Greek word for "fifty": *Pentecost.*

On the first Pentecost after Jesus' death and resurrection, the waiting disciples received the

"The Ascension of Christ"

promised gift of the Holy Spirit (Acts 2:1-4). Then Peter preached to the pilgrims assembled in Jerusalem for the Feast of Pentecost. Peter's message convinced many persons to stake their lives on Jesus and his good news and to become God's new people (Acts 2:37-42). These events have caused Christians to consider Pentecost the "birthday" of the church.

Filled With the Holy Spirit

Read Acts 2:1-4. Luke employs vivid imagery to describe what happened to the first group of Christians on the day of Pentecost when the Holy Spirit came upon them.

Note carefully the language Luke uses in his description. Luke is not saying that the Holy Spirit was present in audible wind and visible fire. He does say, however, that an unearthly sound *"like the rush of a violent wind"* filled the house. Likewise, something that shot forth from a common source and yet was discernible in individual portions *"as of fire"* was among the disciples as a whole and yet came upon them individually.

Luke is relying on the language of metaphor to describe the indescribable. The disciples experienced something that human words fail completely to convey.

Something happened to the disciples that day. Let there be no mistake about that. The two certain things that can be said about this visitation by the Holy Spirit are that (1) it was unearthly, being of God and (2) it gave the disciples real power to begin witnessing to any whom they might encounter.

"Pentecost," from a twelfth-century English illustrated manuscript

What's in a Name?

Christianity has traditionally talked about God being one being who is manifested in three persons. This teaching is known as the doctrine of the Trinity. The three persons of God are God as the Father, God as the Son, and God as the *Holy Spirit*. The Holy Spirit is the least understood by most modern, western Protestants.

You have already read a little about the Holy Spirit in Acts 2. Some of the other New Testament passages that talk about the Holy Spirit are

Mark 1:4-13
John 14:15-17, 25-26
Romans 8:26-27
1 Corinthians 12:1-13
Galatians 5:22-26

The First Christian Sermon

Peter's sermon to the people gathered in Jerusalem on the first Christian Pentecost contained the main points Christians wanted to make as they witnessed about Jesus:

1. Our excitement comes from God's Spirit.

2. Jesus accomplished many marvelous deeds and signs by God's power.

3. Jews and non-Jews (Gentiles—"those outside the law") killed Jesus, though Jesus' death was part of God's intentional plan.

4. God raised Jesus from the dead and exalted him, making him "both Lord and Messiah" (Acts 2:36).

5. Those who would respond to this message about Jesus and accept him as Lord and Messiah are to "repent, and be baptized every one of you in the name of Jesus Christ so that your sins may be forgiven; and you will receive the gift of the Holy Spirit" (Acts 2:38).

6. This message is not just for Jews but for all persons everywhere. All can become God's new people.

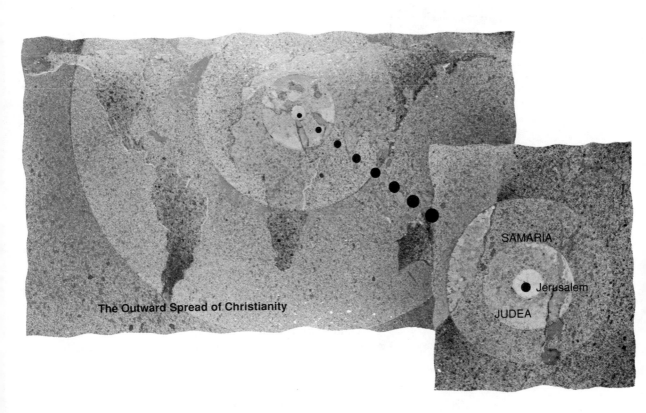

The Outward Spread of Christianity

SAMARIA

● Jerusalem

JUDEA

Site of Simon Peter's house in Capernaum

Stone relief of a Roman ship such as Paul might have sailed on

Aqueduct at Caesarea, where Cornelius lived

Changes From Enemies Into Followers

The Book of the Acts of the Apostles is a book about conversions. Conversion simply means changing from one thing into another. In the case of Christian conversion, a person changes from a condition of either ignorance of or enmity toward God to a condition of desiring to grow increasingly trustful of God.

Though there are many conversions mentioned in Acts, the conversions of three persons in particular are dramatic: Peter, Saul, and Cornelius.

Peter—Acts 2:1-42—cowardly disciple who fearfully denied any relationship with Jesus in order to avoid his own possible arrest—obediently remained with the other disciples in Jerusalem and thereby received the Holy Spirit—boldly began to preach in Christ's name, willingly suffering arrest; became one of the leaders of the early church

Saul (also known by his Roman name, Paul)—Acts 9:1-22—strict Jew who zealously persecuted Christians for blasphemy; involved in the execution of the Christian Stephen—had an encounter with the risen Jesus while on his way to persecute the Christians of Damascus—abrupt about-face from zealous persecutor of Christians to zealous missionary on behalf of Christ; spread the Christian message to much of the non-Jewish European world

Cornelius—Acts 10—a centurion (a major officer) in the Roman army who was sympathetic to the Jewish religion—God sent Peter to speak with Cornelius in response to Cornelius's prayer—received baptism and the Holy Spirit; demonstrated that Gentiles (non-Jews), even those who were part of the hated occupation forces, were legitimate candidates for conversion to Christianity

Marks of the Church (According to Acts 2:43-47)

The people who make up the church—God's new people
—come together;
—have all things in common;
—distribute proceeds from sale of possessions to those in need;
—spend much time together in worship;
—break bread (share in Communion);
—praise God.

What Do I Need to Do to Be a Christian?

1 Renounce the spiritual forces of wickedness, reject the evil powers of this world, and repent of your sins.

2 Accept the freedom and power God gives you to resist evil, injustice, and oppression in whatever forms they present themselves.

3 Confess Jesus Christ as your Savior, put your whole trust in his grace, and promise to serve him as your Lord, in union with the church that Christ has opened to people of all ages, nations, and races.

4 Be baptized in the name of God the Father, the Son, and the Holy Spirit.

5 Faithfully participate in and financially support the ministries of the church.

Read It for Yourself

Read Acts 16. As you read this chapter make notes about the activities and characters of these persons:

Paul—

Timothy—

Lydia—

the jailer—

What do these four persons tell you about being a Christian?

Let the Bible Form You

In each of the other chapters of this book, you have used a psalm to let the Bible form you within. In this chapter, however, you will encounter a different part of the Bible.

When Peter preached the first Christian sermon, he used for his text a portion of Old Testament prophecy: Joel 2:28-32. We do not know much about the prophet Joel, except that it is likely he lived in Judah after the return from the Exile. He called the people to repentance and warned of the coming "day of the LORD," when human beings would be judged by God. Joel described that day as "great and terrible" (Joel 2:31). However, he said the faithful may take comfort that "everyone who calls on the name of the LORD shall be saved" (verse 32).

Find a quiet place to sit for a while. Read Joel 2:28-32 and Acts 2:17-21. Do not worry if there are a few places where Peter changes the words of the Joel passage as he recites them.

In which category mentioned by Joel do you place yourself? Child? Older adult? Young adult? An oppressed person? Any member of humanity (all flesh)? In which way does Joel say God's Spirit will come to you? In an outpouring? In prophecy? In dreams? In visions?

As information, you might find it interesting to know that prophecies, dreams, and visions were all ways in which God spoke directly to persons in the Old Testament. Joel is looking ahead to a time when God will speak to all humanity through God's Spirit.

In *prophecy* persons are especially sensitive to what God's will is for a particular time and place.

In *dreams* God's Spirit works on a person's subconscious while he or she is sleeping.

In *visions* God helps persons to see that reality should be viewed and interpreted through the lens of faith, rather than in the fashion the world sees.

You cannot force prophecies, dreams, and visions to come to you. They are, after all, gifts of the Spirit. They happen as God wills. But you may become more open to God filling you with God's Spirit.

Try this:

- As with other times when you have sought the Scripture to form you within, allow yourself to become quiet inside. Let the noise around you pass you by.
- Ask God to help you to be open to God's Spirit.
- Read Joel 2:28-32 once, twice, even three times. Allow its words and images to wash over you. Do not worry about your mind understanding what is being said. Instead, imagine the words sinking into your heart.
- Allow yourself to wait quietly and patiently for God's Spirit to work within you. Permit yourself at least five minutes in silence. If you must think about anything, think about the words of this Scripture passage. Imagine yourself prophesying, dreaming, envisioning.
- Again, do not expect anything to happen during this time. Simply open yourself to God's Spirit. The Holy Spirit will do what it wants when it wants.
- When the time comes for you to move back into the world, close your time by humming or singing "Spirit, Now Live in Me," printed below.

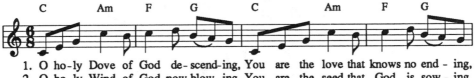

1. O ho-ly Dove of God de-scend-ing, You are the love that knows no end - ing,
2. O ho-ly Wind of God now blow-ing, You are the seed that God is sow - ing,
3. O ho-ly Rain of God now fall - ing, You make the Word of God en-thrall-ing,
4. O ho-ly Flame of God now burn- ing, You are the pow'r of Christ re-turn - ing,

all of our shat-tered dreams you're mend-ing: Spir-it, now live in me. ___
you are the life that starts us grow-ing: Spir-it, now live in me. ___
you are the in - ner voice now call - ing: Spir-it, now live in me. ___
you are the an - swer to our yearn-ing: Spir-it, now live in me. ___

CHAPTER 7

GOD
CALLS US
TO
LIVE
IN
HOPE

In this chapter you will

- think about what faith might mean when you are faced with trouble
- explore some of the kinds of encouragement the Bible offers Christians in trouble
- look for avenues of hope and faith in your life

A Christian Balance Sheet

By this time in your overview of the Bible, you have gained some understanding of what the Bible says the life of a Christian is like. In the space below list some of the benefits of being a Christian and some of the things you might either have to give or have to give up to be a Christian.

What You Get	What You Give or Give Up

How does the weight of what you get by being a Christian compare with what you give?

Images of Christian Commitment

Read 2 Timothy 2:1-13. Second Timothy is a letter written by an older, experienced missionary to a younger, new co-worker. Along with First Timothy and Titus, the letter is filled with advice for a new generation of church leaders.

Second Timothy 2:3-6 contains three images to help Timothy see what the life of a completely committed Christian might look like.

SOLDIER—aims only at pleasing the commander; not concerned with everyday affairs; focuses only on mission as a soldier

ATHLETE—competes only according to the rules; focuses only on winning the champion's crown

FARMER—works diligently in the field for the sake of the first share of the crops

Titus adds that the Christian is not left alone in the struggle to live the committed life: "For the grace of God has appeared, bringing salvation to all, training us to renounce impiety and worldly passions, and in the present age to live lives that are self-controlled, upright, and godly, while we wait for the blessed hope and the manifestation of the glory of our great God and Savior, Jesus Christ" (Titus 2:11-13).

The Last Book

No book of the Bible raises more questions and causes more confusion than the last one—the Book of Revelation. Filled with strange imagery, this book almost did not make it into the Bible. However, its message brought hope to a generation of persecuted Christians: **God reigns supreme!**

> "Blessed is anyone who endures temptation. Such a one has stood the test and will receive the crown of life that the Lord has promised to those who love him."
>
> (James 1:12)

Be careful as you read the Book of Revelation. Its symbols and imagery made sense to its first readers. However, if we try to force those same symbols and images to fit our ways of making sense of reality, we are misusing the book.

The first readers of the Book of Revelation lived in the Roman province of Asia Minor (modern Turkey) during the last years of the first century.

What's in a Name?

The writer of Hebrews provides us with a list of names of faithful people of God. Some of these persons you have already met in the pages of this book. You can learn more about them and meet the others by reading the passages given.

Abel: Hebrews 11:4—Because of his faith, he offered a more acceptable sacrifice than his brother, Cain, offered.—Genesis 4:3-10

Enoch: Hebrews 11:5—He did not experience death because "he had pleased God."—Genesis 5:21-24

Noah: Hebrews 11:7—He respected God's warning about the coming flood.—Genesis 6:13-22

Abraham: Hebrews 11:8-12, 17-19—He obeyed God when God called him to set out for a place he did not know. He considered God to be faithful. He was ready to sacrifice his only son to God.—Genesis 12:1-8; 15:5-6; 17:19; 18:11-14; 21:2; 22:1-10, 17; 32:12

Isaac: Hebrews 11:20—He invoked blessings upon the futures of his sons, Jacob and Esau.—Genesis 27:27-29, 39-40

Jacob: Hebrews 11:21—He blessed each of the sons of Joseph, trusting the future even when he

Joseph: himself was dying.—Genesis 48:8-20
Hebrews 11:22—He looked ahead to the Exodus when he was dying.—Genesis 50:24-25; Exodus 13:19

Moses: Hebrews 11:23-28—He chose to share the ill treatment suffered by the Hebrews rather than to enjoy the privileges of the Egyptians. He also held on to courage while leaving Egypt and observing the first Passover.—Exodus 2; 12:21-30

Rahab: Hebrews 11:31—She was a prostitute of Jericho who survived its destruction because she hid two Israelite spies.—Joshua 2:1-21; 6:22-25

Gideon, Barak, Samson, Jephthah, David, Samuel: Hebrews 11:32-34—They conquered kingdoms; administered justice; obtained the fulfillment of promises; escaped death by wild animals, fire, and sword; and achieved victories in battle although militarily weaker.—Judges 4–8; 11; 13–16; 1 Samuel 1–30; 2 Samuel; 1 Kings 1–2

Jesus: Hebrews 12:2, 24— He endured the cross and is considered "the pioneer and perfecter of our faith," "the mediator of a new covenant."

At that time, the Roman Emperor Domitian claimed to be a god. He called upon all the inhabitants of the empire, including the inhabitants of Asia Minor, to worship him. Christians refused. Christians claimed that only the God revealed in Jesus Christ was to be worshiped.

Many Christians were therefore treated as enemies of the state. The authorities considered them guilty of the crimes of atheism and treason. They were arrested, imprisoned, tortured, and executed.

To provide comfort and hope to these frightened and suffering Christians, John recorded his visions of the ultimate sovereignty and the final triumph of God over all evil, whether worldly or spiritual. Instead of finding comfort in the Revelation of John, however, some persons have instead been frightened by its fearsome imagery. They find in John's words not hope but the doom of the end of the world. Nevertheless, the true message of Revelation is that God will reign gloriously throughout eternity and will share that reign with those who remain faithful.

Glimpses of Eternity

The most important of the visions John shared in his Revelation are those found in Revelation 21:1–22:6. Read those verses through; then record your impressions in the box in the margin.

You were probably able to appreciate the beauty of John's language. However, some of John's meanings would have been far more clear to his first readers than they are to you.

For one thing, his first-century readers would have had a more thorough knowledge of some of the obscure images used by John and taken from the Old Testament. For another, those readers might have been accustomed to reading materials with similar images and intent. Finally, John's readers would have lived in the midst of danger and suffering. The Revelation spoke directly to their situation.

For example, when you read Revelation 21:15-16, you found it describing the heavenly city of the New Jerusalem as a perfect cube. Did you know that 1 Kings 6:20 describes the holy of holies within the Temple in the earthly city of Jerusalem as a room with equal dimensions for length, depth, and height—a cube?

The holy of holies was the place within the Temple where God was thought to be present as in no other place on the whole earth. When Revelation 21:22 proceeded to tell the first readers

The angel with the key hurls the dragon into the abyss, and another angel shows John the New Jerusalem (Revelation 20:1-3; 21:9-12; 22:8).

Impressions:

that the New Jerusalem had no temple at all, they would have realized that the New Jerusalem had no need for a temple. It was itself a perfect sanctuary—the place for humanity to meet God. And those readers would have quickly realized that the New Jerusalem was not literally a city but rather the church existing as the gathered people of God.

When you read Revelation 21:19-20, did you puzzle over the listing of precious gems said to adorn the foundations of the wall of the city? Why that much detail? Did you pass quickly on to a more "sensible" portion of the text?

The first readers would have realized that those same jewels were found in the breastplate of the high priest (Exodus 28:17-21; 39:10-14). They evoked a sense of the immediacy of God's presence.

As you read Revelation 22:4, did you merely think how nice it was that God's people would see God's face? Did you make the connection with Exodus 33:17-23, where the greatest religious figure of Judaism—Moses—only was permitted to see the back of God because God's holiness was so pure it would have killed him?

The explanations of these references are not intended to make you feel inadequate as a student of the Bible. First, you need to realize that Bible study is a lifelong process. You are only now in the beginning stages of learning. Keep at it! Have patience! Work at it!

Second, these explanations, and others you might find in a commentary or study Bible, can help you realize that reading the Bible—especially a book like Revelation—is truly a cross-cultural experience. You cannot expect to know the customs, language, and patterns of meaning familiar to persons from another time, place, and culture.

Third, you do share your Christianity in common with the first readers of Revelation. Like them, you are trying to become more faithful to your Lord, Jesus Christ. As you struggle to understand Revelation and other portions of Scripture, you look forward to the day of God's final victory and live in hope.

Finally, you might find it helpful to think of the Bible as offering a set of lenses through which to view reality, instead of always seeing reality through the lenses the world insists upon. What looks different because you are a Christian and live in hope? That insight might help you appreciate better what Revelation has to say.

The island of Patmos where John was imprisoned when he wrote the Book of Revelation

You Won't Find *That* In Heaven!

Perhaps more important than all the gilded imagery of Revelation 21–22 to those who are seeking comfort and hope is John's description of what will *not* be found when we stand in the presence of God.

21:1	no sea	There will be no chaotic force of "un-creation," which is the opposite of God's being and creating, loose in the world.
21:4	no tears, death, sorrow, crying, pain	Life will be abundantly full.
21:8	no persons who are cowardly, faithless, or impure; no murderers, fornicators, sorcerers, idolaters, or liars	The city that is filled with God's presence will be freed and empty of the sins that infect the present world. (Note that these sins were specifically those found either in the pagan cults and the emperor worship that surrounded the late first-century Christians or in the actions of former Christians who renounced their faith out of fear of persecution.)
21:22	no temple	The entire city is holy with God's immediate presence.
21:23, 25; 22:5	no sun, moon, night, or closed gates	God is light. Therefore, there is no darkness nor any of the fears or anxieties associated with the darkness.
22:3	no curse	The curse pronounced on the occasion of the first sin (Genesis 3:17) will be no more.

Read It for Yourself

Read 1 Peter 1:1-9.

Focus on verse 2. Think back over the previous chapters of this book in which you have encountered some of the themes mentioned in this verse. In what other Bible stories have you considered what it means to be

Chosen?

Sanctified (made holy) by the Holy Spirit?

Obedient?

Sprinkled with blood?

What have you learned from those other Bible stories that helps you to understand this passage? Review those previous stories briefly if you need to.

Now, focus on verses 3-9. What is being offered? What do you have to do to receive what is offered?

Let the Bible Form You

Find a quiet place, and permit yourself to become quiet inside to the best of your ability. Read Psalm 103 silently or aloud.

One scholar has called Psalm 103 "one of the finest blossoms on the tree of biblical faith" (Artur Weiser, *The Psalms: A Commentary*, Westminster Press, 1962; page 657). Another scholar has observed how the poet of this psalm begins by noting God's saving actions for the individual (verses 3-5). Next the psalmist moves on to describe God's saving actions for the whole community of faith (verses 6-18). Finally, the psalmist looks to God's activity on behalf of the entire universe (verses 19-22) (Bernhard W. Anderson, *Out of the Depths: The Psalms Speak for Us Today*, revised and expanded edition, Westminster Press, 1983; pages 128–29).